The exhibition is presented through the
combined efforts of the City of
Philadelphia, the Republic of Chile,
the Philadelphia Regional Port Authority,
the Chilean & American Chamber of
Commerce of Greater Philadelphia,
the Delaware River Port Authority,
the Port of History Museum and the
Chilean Museum of Precolumbian Art,
with valuable assistance from
numerousAmerican and Chilean business
and civic leaders.

COVER: Woman in formal
attire (nineteenth century).
Drawing and computer
design by José Pérez de Arce.

MAPUCHE

SEEDS OF THE CHILEAN SOUL

AN EXHIBIT AT THE PORT OF HISTORY MUSEUM
AT PENN'S LANDING
PHILADELPHIA, PENNSYLVANIA

MARCH 27 - JUNE 30, 1992

MUSEO CHILENO DE ARTE PRECOLOMBINO
CITY OF PHILADELPHIA
COMISION NACIONAL CHILE V CENTENARIO

SPONSORS

Commonwealth of Pennsylvania
C.S.A.V. - Chilean Lines
Fidelity Bank
SmithKline Beecham

PATRONS

City of Philadelphia
Embassy of Chile
Philadelphia Regional Port Authority
I. Municipalidad de Santiago
Fundacion Familia Larrain Echenique
Comision Nacional Preparatoria Chile V Centenario
Independent Pier Company
Pepper Hamilton & Scheetz
Ladeco Airlines
Seagate Corporation
The Friends of the Museums
Delaware River Port Authority
Chiquita-Frupac
Wolf D. Barth
Maritrans

FRIENDS

Western Fumigation
Australia & New Zealand Banking Group Ltd.
Pennsylvania Humanities Council
Banco Sudamericano
Curtis, Mallet-Prevost, Colt & Mosel
First National Bank of Maryland
Gilmartin, Poster & Shafto
Holt Cargo
Kirlin, Campbell & Keating
Lepon McCarthy Jutkowitz & Holzworth
Maddy, Dalton & Lion
International Longshoremen Association
Philadelphia Marine Trade Association
Suma Fruit International
Universal Maritime Service Corporation
Unifrutti of America
Sunny Valley International Inc.
CIA. Chilena de Navegacion Interoceánica
Garden State Freezers
Quality Sales
Jac Vandenberg, Inc.
Miciak & Company
Penn International
Agrimar USA Incorporation
Palmer Biezup & Henderson
Phillyship
Penn Trucking & Warehouse Inc.

CONTENTS

The organizers of *Mapuche: Seeds of The Chilean Soul* gratefully acknowledge the generous support of the General Assembly of the Commonwealth of Pennsylvania in the production of this catalogue. In particular, gratitude is expressed to the Honorable Vincent J. Fumo, a member of the Senate of Pennsylvania for his support and encouragement of this project.

Throughout its 300-year history, the City of Philadelphia has welcomed visitors from around the world. The City's founder, William Penn, conceived Philadelphia and Pennsylvania as a place congenial to diverse peoples and cultures. He had the generosity of vision to recognize that a community that welcomed diverse influences would grow and thrive.

As the Mayor of William Penn's city, I take great pride in welcoming to Philadelphia the exhibition *Mapuche: Seeds of the Chilean Soul.*

This exhibit marks several milestones. It represents the first time this unique collection of historic artifacts from Chile's most important indigenous ethnic group has left the world-famous Museo Chileno de Arte Precolombino in Santiago, Chile for exhibition abroad. Though we are celebrating this year the 500th anniversary of the Western World's encounter with the Americas, this collection of exquisite silverwork, weavings, ceramics and other artifacts reminds us of the advanced and thriving cultures that had already laid the foundation of the multi-cultural richness we enjoy in this part of the world.

More importantly, however, this exhibition deepens the relationship between the Republic of Chile and the Commonwealth of Pennsylvania's international seaport here in Philadelphia. This relationship began more than twenty years ago with the importation of Chilean agricultural products into our port. It has since grown from a modest beginning to the point that Philadelphia has become the primary port in the United States for the importation of Chile's agricultural products. With the opening of this exhibit that examines the past and present culture of Chile's ancient Mapuche peoples, I am pleased to say this important economic relationship now has a cultural dimension, as well, one that will grow in future years with other exhibits both here and in Chile.

I am gratified that you are here for this exciting exhibit and this important new beginning. Many people should be thanked for their efforts in bringing *Mapuche: Seeds of the Chilean Soul* to Philadelphia. I am especially grateful to the Chilean and American Chamber of Commerce of Greater Philadelphia, the Philadelphia Regional Port Authority, the Delaware River Port Authority, the City of Philadelphia through its Department of Commerce, Chilean Lines, the Port of History Museum, and the other numerous sponsors, all who gave their time and money to make this exhibit a reality.

This exhibit has been over four years in the making. Its doors are now open, allowing you to view cultural artifacts never before seen in the United States. I know you will always remember this visit.

All the best,

EDWARD G. RENDELL
Mayor of Philadelphia

THE HONORARY COMMITEE FOR THE EXHIBITION

Committee Chairman:
William R. Klaus
    Partner
    Pepper Hamilton & Scheetz
Honorable Robert P. Casey
    Governor
    Commonwealth of Pennsylvania
Honorable Edward G. Rendell
    Mayor
    City of Philadelphia
His Excellency Patricio Silva
    Ambassador of Chile to the United States
Charles P. Pizzi
    President
    Greater Philadelphia Chamber of Commerce
Roland K. Bullard
    President
    Fidelity Bank
Henry Wendt
    Chairman of the Board
    SmithKline Beecham
Ricardo Claro
    Chairman
    Compañia Sud Americana de Vapores S.A.
Reverend Nicholas S. Rashford S.J.
    Chairman
    Delaware River Port Authority
Wallace H. Nunn
    Chairman
    Philadelphia Regional Port Authority
Marcel Jeanneret
    President
    Chilean American Chamber of Commerce
    of Greater Philadelphia

MESSAGE FROM THE AMBASSADOR OF CHILE
TO THE UNITED STATES

In Philadelphia, and around the world, Chile has become known for its dynamic trade activity. This is only one of the country's most fascinating characteristics.

Mapuche: Seeds of the Chilean Soul is part of an important effort to present a broader picture of our nation's past and present.

The Mapuche developed a complex culture in pre-Hispanic times that withstood the onslaught of European traditions and lived on into the modern world. Today their culture forms a fundamental part of Chile's broad cultural heritage.

I would like to express the gratitude of the Government of Chile for the support of the City of Philadelphia and the Commonwealth of Pennsylvania, and for the cooperation of the many corporations and individuals in Chile and the United States all of whom have contributed to making this exhibit possible.

The City of Brotherly Love, where Chilean and United States businessmen have built a strong trade relationship, is an especially appropriate location to host the Museo Chileno de Arte Precolombino's first overseas exhibition.

I invite you all to enjoy the exhibit. I hope the exhibit, and this book, offer you meaningful insights into the culture of the Mapuche people and encourage you to find out more about Chile.

PATRICIO SILVA
Ambassador of Chile

EXHIBITION CURATOR: Carlos Aldunate del Solar
EXHIBITION DESIGNER: José Pérez de Arce
GRAPHIC DESIGN: José Pérez de Arce
TYPESETTING: Ken Getz Design Associates
MANNEQUINS: Ken Getz Design Associates
COORDINATION IN PHILADELPHIA: Ronald Barber and Corliss Cavalieri
PUBLIC RELATIONS: Resnick Communications Inc.
INSTALLATION: Luis Solar and Manuel Raimán

Wooden horse courtesy of 1st Troop Philadelphia City Cavalry.

MESSAGE FROM THE MUSEO CHILENO DE ARTE PRECOLOMBINO

It is a honor and a privilege for the Museo Chileno de Arte Precolombino to present this exhibition - the first the museum has assembled for the United States of America - on the Mapuche people, the largest indigenous group in Chile and a determining element in our national character.

According to the earliest historical records, when the Spanish Conquistadors reached this corner of the Americas, the Mapuche language was spoken over most of present-day Chile. The main colonial and republican settlements were established in Mapuche territory, causing them to become the aboriginal seed of the Chilean people. Expressions of this heritage can still be found in the the names of many of Chile's lakes, mountains, rivers and other places, in some coloquial terms, and in our local cuisine. Above all, Mapuche heritage is kept alive by nearly half a million people who still cherish their ancestral traditions, and in the mixed blood of most Chileans.

Following a brief introduction to the prehistory of those who occupied the southern forests from the seventh century onward, the exhibition focuses in the present day and recent-past ethnography of the Mapuche. Early Mapuche history is marked by the fighting of these people to defend their territory: first, against the Inca, then the Spaniards, and finally, the armies of the emergent Republic of Chile, which incorporated these lands into the national domain late in the last century.
This protracted war experience, in a large measure, forged Mapuche culture.

Mapuche everyday life will become palpable through a visit to a life-sized replica of their dwelling, or *ruka*, filled of its usual household articles. A hint of their cosmology will be provided by the reproduction of a Mapuche cementery and elements of their rich shamanic activities. Finally, large wall prints, videos and music will recreate their landscape and their language, key to the social cohesion of this native people.

This exhibit is sponsored by the City of Philadelphia, the Philadelphia and Delaware Port Authorities, and the Chilean National Comitee of Conmemoration of the Quincentenary Aniversary, to whom we wish to express our deepest appreciation. We would also like to thank the companies and individuals, both in Chile and the United States of America, who so generously provided their financial support.

SERGIO LARRAIN GARCIA MORENO
President, Museo Chileno de Arte Precolombino

MAPUCHE
SEEDS OF THE CHILEAN SOUL

CARLOS ALDUNATE DEL SOLAR
DIRECTOR, MUSEO CHILENO DE ARTE PRECOLOMBINO

This publication, a first in the English language, is an expanded version of the book *Cultura Mapuche*, third
edition (1986) published by the Ministerio de Educación de Chile and the Museo Chileno de Arte Precolombino.

Cementery (XIX century). Photograph courtesy of Museo Histórico Nacional.

I saw the Indians, their houses
with humble walls and roofs,
the trees and plants were tilled,
the fruits, the seeds, the greenery;
important things in them I gathered
rituals, ceremonies and manners,
how they treated and exercised each other,
the law and order under which they lived

The simple people of these lands
with their honest kindness and endearments
showed neatly that cupidity
had not yet entered in those wilderness
nor stealing, wickedness, injustice,
the ordinary nourishment of wars,
had gained an entrance to these sites,
natural law had not been defiled.

But then ourselves destroying
everything that we touched as we passed by
with our usual insolence trespassing
gave them roomy entrance and ample room
corrupting ancient custom
debased by new contempts,
and here set its flag cupidity
much more firmly than anywhere else.

FROM THE CHANT XXXII OF THE EPIC POEM "LA ARAUCANA",
BY DON ALONSO DE ERCILLA Y ZUÑIGA (XVI CENTURY).

INTRODUCTION

In the Americas there are still native peoples - the last representatives of those indigenous ethnic groups who, through the millennia, populated these continents, conquering jungles, deserts, vast beaches and soaring mountains. In the struggle to survive, they developed a thorough understanding of the climate, flora and fauna of the different territories they inhabited. Some of these groups domesticated plants and animals, developing complex agricultural and herding economies, at times reaching the level of State organizations. Other, more isolated groups, perhaps less challenged by their environments, maintained hunting and gathering economies for long periods of time.

The European invasion was so overwhelming, its effects so dramatic, that in less than a century, the ethnic face of the continent changed completely. Today, indigenous groups are minorities in American countries. The majority society, generally mestizo, has adopted western, Christian cultural customs. It is difficult, to say the least, for these ethnic minorities to compete in the majority society, with which they have legitimate conflicts of interest. As a result, they have been relegated to a position of inferiority, usually occupying lands of poor quality or of little value, and are beset by economic and health problems. Worse, a serious cultural erosion has taken place due to the imposition of values and ways of life that are alien to their traditional systems.

Ensuring the survival of these peoples in the industrial world poses a serious challenge for the social sciences. A position must be found, a role for them to play within national development plans which fully respects their cultural uniqueness and takes advantage of the admirable symbiosis they have attained with their natural environment. The loss of their cultural values and identities would constitute irreparable damage to the heritage of humanity itself.

Chile is privileged to have an indigenous ethnic group with half million members which, in pre-Hispanic times, occupied the south central part of the country. The descendants of that group, who mixed with Europeans, gave rise to the Chilean nationality.

It was the custom of the Spanish conquerors to name indigenous groups for the places they inhabited. Thus the inhabitants of the area of Arauco, one of the principal indigenous "provinces," came to be called "Araucanos."

The first to use that name more generically to designate all the indigenous peoples who inhabited the south of Chile to Chiloé was Alonso de Ercilla in his monumental epic poem *La Araucana*. Perhaps for this reason the name became popularized. It was used up to the present era to designate all the Indian groups who spoke the **Mapuche** language. Due to the imprecision of the term Araucano and fundamentally out of respect for the peoples themselves, today it is considered more appropriate to refer to them by the name **Mapuche** ("people of the land"), the word they themselves use.

THE MAPUCHE
AND THEIR LAND

Kuifi ta ché mëte kimniefui
kom elechi weshakelu
Kimenmaniefui ñi üi
wenumapu Wilëfükechi
wanël en kom feichi üñem
Üpenkiawi piuchill meu
tëfachi naqmapu miauchi
kulliñ ka feichi kakeume
ishike Keyü pululeufü, lafken
rume, weyeliaukechi challwa
Kä kimniefui kom mawida
ka kachu Keyü tëfachi kura
üineumejui .

Travelling toward the east.

The ancient Mapuche
were on intimate terms
with all things.
They had names for the
stars that shone
in the heavenly vault, the birds that
flew through the air,
the animals that walked on
the land, and the insects.
Even the fishes that
swam in the rivers
and the sea.
They also knew all about
the trees and the grasses.
They even had names for the stones.

(PASCUAL COÑA IN WILHELM DE MOESBACH, 1930)

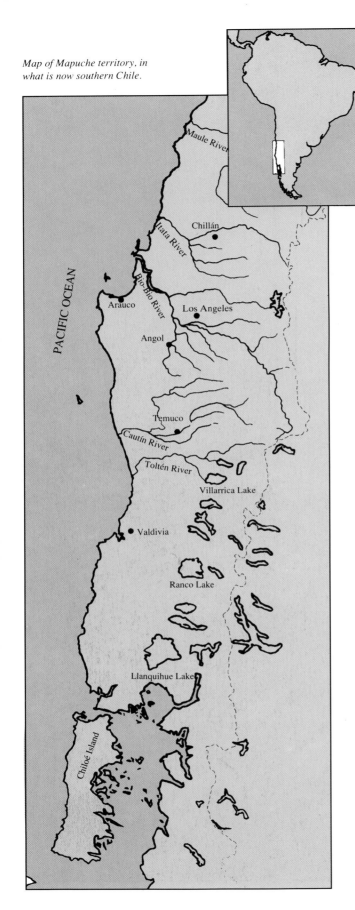

Map of Mapuche territory, in what is now southern Chile.

The first chroniclers who described the recently conquered territory of Chile noted that south of the Itata River there was a drastic change in climate, flora and fauna, accompanied by an increase in the Indian population. The beech (**Nothofagus**) forests, which began in the mountainous regions further north, dominated the entire region south of the Itata, from the coastal plains to the mountains, where they yielded to the "araucarias" (native conifers). The beech forests *(hualo, hualli, pellín and coigüe)* created areas that were particularly favorable for human settlement. They and their associated shrubs, herbs and fungi produced great quantities of berries, fruits and other woodland food resources. In addition, as deciduous trees, they allowed the sun to heat the soil during the autumn and winter, thus impeding the formation of humid swampland - poor environments for human habitation.

Proceeding south from the Rio Cautín region (39ºS) environmental conditions were not as beneficent. Human settlement became more difficult due to increasing evergreen (laurifoliate) forests and precipitation. As a result, sites were confined to

*In the foothills of the **inapire mapu**, are a series of glacial lakes. Here, early signs of Indian occupation can be found (C. Aldunate).*

certain ecological niches, particularly the central valley and the piedmont region. The coastal region, which includes a mountain range and a rugged shoreline, both covered with dense, impentetrable vegetation, was especially unfavorable for human occupation. Farther south, on the island of Chiloé is the last surviving enclave of people who speak *mapudungu* (the "language of the land").

For the Mapuche, these territories were divided into several culturally important zones, referred to with special names in their language.

The Andes Mountains , or Cordillera - pire mapu ("land of the snows") - are lower in those latitudes than in the central or northern part of present- day Chile. Featuring numerous mountain passes, the Southern Andes can be easily crossed to reach the eastern slopes and the adjacent "pampas." As in other parts of pre-Hispanic America, this snowy highland, far from constituting a barrier between peoples, was in fact a meeting place for the diverse Mapuche, Pehuenche and Puelche peoples who inhabited the eastern and western slopes of the

Inapire mapu, *or "land close to the snow." View of volcanoes through beech (Nothofagus) forest (M. Thomas).*

Mapuche settlement on the Central valley plains, or lelfun mapu (N. Piwonka).

Gathering **luche** *sea weed*
(***Ulva lactuca***), *on the coast*
(*M. Thomas*).

Cordillera. From that contact, based upon an exchange of manufactured goods, animals and women, came a strong mixture of ethnic groups and the beginning of the diffusion of Mapuche culture toward the Argentine pampas.

Dense natural forest dominated by *pewen* (**Araucaria araucana**, a native conifer), characterize the western slopes of the Cordillera - *inapire mapu* ("land close to the snows"). Pine cones from the *pewen* constituted the principal food of the Pehuenche ("pine people"), hunter-gatherers who roamed the territory living off the abundant flora and fauna of the region, braving the rigors of its climate and descending to the plains during the summer with animals, pine cones, salt and rough leather goods to exchange for agricultural, textile and manufactured articles provided by the Mapuche. At times such incursions occasioned raids and assaults during which the Pehuenche carried off women and other prizes of war. It was through the Pehuenche that the Argentine pampas became "Araucanized," so that by the end of the last century, the Mapuche language unified the aboriginal population inhabiting those latitudes from the Pacific to the Atlantic Ocean.

With a large portion of the natural forests having disappeared from the region, the Andean slopes are now used by the Mapuche as pasturage and, in some cases, for logging. Gathering continues to play a primary role in the subsistence of the indigenous groups of the area. The annual "piñón" or pine nut harvest falls into this category. The pine nuts, which are stored underground, provide the Mapuche with a vital raw material used in preparing flour, drinks and other food products.

The *lelfun mapu* ("land of the plains") has excellent agricultural potential. Indigenous settlements were established on the banks of the region's innumerable streams and rivers. Attracted by the favorable conditions, most of the country's Indians settled in this region. The temperate climate produced by the enclosure of the area between two mountain ranges was a contributing factor. The heavy vegetation which originally covered the plains was removed by the Mapuche beginning in pre-Hispanic times to establish their settlements, small orchards and rudimentary agricultural activities. The vastness and richness of the arable soils made it possible for groups to move from place to place in search of new territories to occupy.

Since the end of the past century, the Mapuche have occupied land ceded to their ancestors by the Chilean State. These reservations caused them to lose their semi-mobile lifestyle and to establish fixed settlements. With the steady growth of these settlements, the land has been subdivided into smaller and smaller units, and available resources have been stretched to the limit. On the other side of the coastal range, which attains its greatest heights in the Nahuelbuta range, is the littoral – *lafken mapu* ("land by the sea"). Soils of poor agricultural quality cause food supply problems for the *lafkenche* ("coastal dweller") aboriginal groups, who have turned to fishing and shellfish gathering to complement their diet. It was the great abundance of fish, shellfish and algae which attracted intense

settlement in the region in prehistoric times, as evidenced by numerous and heavy shell middens found throughout the littoral.

Of extreme importance to the Mapuche's concept of space is *puel mapu* ("land of the East") or *waithif*. The manner in which the indigenous peoples discovered this territory through the powerful vehicle of interchange has already been described, along with the resultant process of racial and cultural mixing. Today, the relation of the Mapuche with the eastern territory takes the form of close family ties and friendships which result in frequent visits by the inhabitants of both sides of the mountains. The ties were strengthened by the successive migrations which resulted from the military campaigns in both territories during the end of the last century. Any situation of danger resulted in the immediate movement of entire groups of Mapuche from one side of the mountains to the other, where they were taken in by their neighbors, who offered them lodging and protection.

Araucaria (N. Piwonka).

THE FOREBEARS

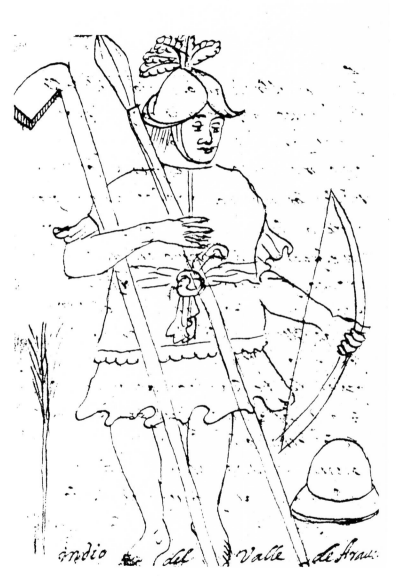

Ñi felemun taiñ pu laku ka
taiñ felemun taiñ pu chau
em, feelyiñ mai taiñ mongelen meu .

First drawings of "Araucanian" Indians in the
chronicles of Fray Diego de Ocaña (1599-1605).

india Araucana   del mismo Valle

Just as our grandparents were,
And our fathers,
We shall be in our life.

(IN PADRE FÉLIX DE AUGUSTA, 1934)

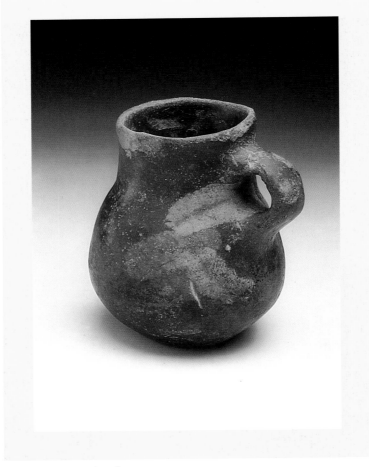

*Jar, or **Metawe**, Pitrén style*
(VII century) Museo Chileno
de Arte Precolombino
(n°1481) (F. Maldonado).

The archeologist scrutinizes the earth for the hidden history of mankind. Anthropologists, geographers and botanists assist him in reconstructing cultural and physical contexts. All are engaged in reconstructing a history which left no written testimony of its own existence, the memory of which has been lost or transformed with the passage of the centuries. That hidden stage in the life of mankind has been called Pre-History. The interest in finding out more about it is based on human nature itself, our basic need to know who we are, where we came from and where we are going.

The origin of the Mapuche people was of great interest to the researchers of the beginning of this century. Some held that the "Araucanian" was a mixture arising as a consequence of the irruption of an ethnic group known as Moluche, warriors and hunters who inhabited the extensive Argentine Pampas and conquered the territory between the Bío-Bío and Toltén rivers in what is now Chile.

Mixing with the more sedentary and agricultural inhabitants of the area, the Moluche were supposed to have destroyed the racial homogeneity which had extended from the Choapa River to Chiloé island, resulting in the creation of three groups: the Picunche, north of the Bío-Bío; the "Araucanos" (a mixed population between the Bío-Bío and Toltén rivers); and the Huilliche, south of the Toltén.

Other researchers rejected such a mixture and argued for the ethnic unity of the Mapuche and their kinship with the northern cultures. Archeological and ethnographic works in recent decades have placed more emphasis on the cultural history of these peoples than on their origins.

Thus a beginning has been made in uncovering a panorama which is richer, more varied and dynamic than was previously thought. We now know that man occupied the rich environments of the littoral for several millennia, making use of the

"Duck-jar", or **Ketru metawe***, Pitrén style (VII century) Museo Chileno de Arte Precolombino (n 2490) (F. Maldonado).*

"Duck-jar" or **Ketru metawe**, *Valdivia style (XVI - XIX centuries), Cristián Bulnes collection, (N. Piwonka).*

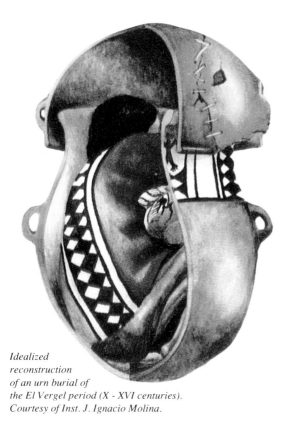

Idealized reconstruction of an urn burial of the El Vergel period (X - XVI centuries). Courtesy of Inst. J. Ignacio Molina.

inexhaustible resources of the sea, complementing them by gathering vegetables and hunting the birds and animals of the region. Toward the middle of the first millennium of the present era, peoples already acquainted with the ceramic arts arrived. They cultivated some agricultural products in small gardens, cleared forests and took advantage of seasonal rains. Archeologists have named those peoples *Pitrén* due to the site where they were first detected. These groups primarily established themselves along the banks of the region's various piedmont lakes, which suggests an economy based on gathering activities. They buried their dead with offerings, such as some well-constructed, well-fired ceramic pitchers, generally in anthropomorphic or zoomorphic shapes, with modellings and incisions and occasionally the remnants of a resistant surface painting.

About five centuries later, human settlements appeared south of the Bío-Bío river, as evidenced

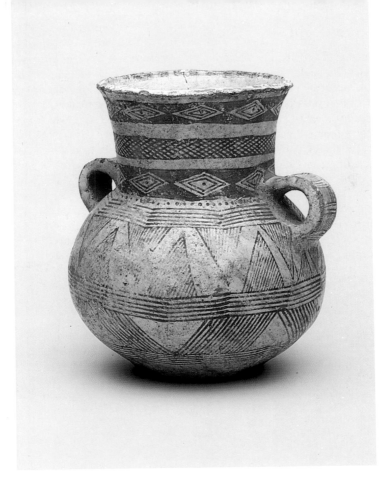

*Jar, or **Metawe**, Valdivia
style (VII - XIX centuries),
Museo Chileno de Arte
Precolombino (nº1429).*

by the burial of children and adults in large ceramic urns accompanied by ceramic offerings painted with red or black lines over a slip - an opaque white finish coating applied to the clay. Sometimes the remains of copper adornments were found as well. These funeral sites occupy river banks in the central valley, and are particularly concentrated in the Angol area, on the Pacific coast. The ancient inhabitants are referred to as **El Vergel**, due to the site where their remains where first discovered. El Vergel people cultivated corn, beans, *dawe* (a small, indigenous grain), chili peppers and pumpkins along the rivers and in swamps, constructing primitive ditches for irrigation. Agricultural specialization by the El Vergel groups is suggested by the location of the cemeteries in what is still one of the most important centers of agriculture in the area, where soils are of superior quality and the Nahuelbuta coastal range provides a kind of protective barrier, inducing a more continental climate.

El Vergel must have had contact with Pitrén, since it has been demonstrated that the two groups existed at the same time, occupying different locations. Also documented is the co-existence in the mountains of hunter and gatherer groups with different cultural traditions.

The impact of the Spanish conquest on these territories produced a sudden and dramatic upheaval in the life of the autochthonous populations which responded to the pressure of conquest with fierce solidarity. One plausible description of the process is that the different peoples who had inhabited the territories united, incorporating ethnic and cultural elements from the mountains and beyond, even from the Spaniards.

This process of real cultural homogenization has come in modern times to be called the Mapuche culture.

Thus, the modern Mapuche people feature a blend of cultural characteristics. Probably their knowledge of how to domesticate plants as well as their caramic tradition came from Pitren, the first Andean peoples with these expertise; their farming tradition and the incipient animal domestication, most likely came from El Vergel; and their herding customs and equestrian culture, as well as some physical traits, are traceable to the Spaniards.

However, there is still much more to learn about the Mapuche's past. Studies of the scant human remains exhumed from ancient cemeteries must be intensified, with more emphasis placed on making stratigraphic excavations and conducting comparative works in the different ecologic niches to assist in casting light on the mysteries that still remain. Unfortunately, the climate in the area is relatively unstable, which has impeded the natural conservation of organic remains. As a result, a large part of the scarce resources so vital for unraveling the prehistoric past of the Mapuche is being lost. On the other hand, researchers have access to the present day descendents who, in spite of foreign influences , still conserve most of their true heritage. A thorough study of their lore and other ethnographic elements ought to more than make up for the lack of archeological information.

Head-shaped axe, probably a symbol of authority (VII century), Museo Chileno de Arte Precolombino. Permanent loan from Mr. Ricardo Irarrázabal (F. Maldonado).

ASCENT AND WAR

Akui mai dengu pu
lonko.
Rangiñ wenu pu lonko.
Shillalen kawell!
Trepenei mai pu kona
Dullipe kümeke kawell,
weupikaiáiñ,
chaliafíiñ mai fentechi
pu lonko.
Ya mai, pu ülmen,
prakawelliñ mai!
Ya mai, sarkéntokona
Ngënékoniaiaimi.

Burial ceremony of **toki** *Cathiji, May 1835. Engraving by Gay (1854).*

Word has come
from the chiefs.
From the chiefs of the
celestial region.
Saddle my horse!
Wake the braves!
Choose the best horses!
we are going to parley,
Greet many chiefs.
Now then, powerful
lords!
Mount your steeds!
Captain, take charge of
your troops!

(IN PADRE FÉLIX DE AUGUSTA, 1934)

Women wearing silver ornaments in the fashion of XVIII-XIX and XX centuries. Drawing by José Pérez de Arce, Museo Chileno de Arte Precolombino.

Mapuche woman's attire (XVIII century), Museo Chileno de Arte Precolombino (N. Piwonka).

During the second half of the fifteenth century, A.D., the Inca incorporated into their extensive empire the meridional territories which became known as *Kolla Suyu* ("Southern Kingdom"). Effective control, however, appears to have extended only as far south as the Maipo river.

Isolated military enclaves beyond that line may have served the function of safeguarding the frontier of the subjugated territories. South of the Maule river, the conquest met fierce resistance from indigenous groups who, taking advantage of the dense forest cover, halted the invading troops and impeded their advance southward. The members of these local groups were called *aukas* or *purun aukas*, which is a Quechua word (the language of the Inca) meaning enemy, rebel or savage.

The Inca thus paved the way for Spanish domination. After the conquest of Cuzco, the Incan administrative and political center, and the submission of its leadership, the empire's nucleus and hierarchical organization facilitated the advance of the Spaniards through all of the controlled territories. The first Spaniards arrived in Chile accompanied by dignitaries of the Inca court to facilitate the transfer of power to the new conquerors. It was precisely on the southern frontier of the empire that they were stopped by the same Aukas or rebels that the Inca had never been able to conquer.

*Mapuche woman's attire
(XIX century), Museo Chileno
de Arte Precolombino
(N.Piwonka).*

Spanish troops commanded by Pedro de Valdivia overcame that resistance and reached the large island of Chiloé in the far south. But they were never able to dominate the land. Successive attacks and indigenous uprisings culminated in the disaster of Curalaba, the destruction of seven southern Spanish cities and the retreat of Spanish forces to the north bank of the Bío-Bío. That boundary was legally recognized during the Parley of Quillín, held on January 6, 1641. The autonomy of the indigenous peoples located south of the Bío-Bío and the independence of those territories was recognized during the entire colonial period and for almost a century after the establishment of the Republic. That period of ongoing hostilities was known as the Arauco War. Spain was obliged to fortify the frontiers and maintain a professional army to defend them, a situation unheard of in the American colonies.

Although the Spaniards were unable to conquer the territories south of the Bío-Bío river because of the stubborn indigenous resistance, the entire region did not react in the same manner toward the invasion. While the Mapuche living between the Bío-Bío and the Toltén defended their independence jealously and did not allow any penetration whatsoever, those south of the Toltén, fewer in number and more divided, allowed the installation of military and missionary enclaves during the second half of the seventeenth century.

Mapuche chieftains in parley with General Cornelio Saavedra (1880). Photograph courtesy of Museo Histórico Nacional.

*Gathering **pewen** (Araucaria araucana), or pine nuts in the Nahuelbuta range (XIX century), engraving by Gay (1854).*

While those establishments did not result in the colonization of the territories in which they were located, they did bring about changes in the way of life of the indigenous groups living in their proximity. Consequently, while the region of Araucanía maintained traditional Mapuche institutions in effect with notable vigor, in Valdivia another social and cultural situation developed, more similar to that existing north of the Bío-Bío, characterized by the creation of pacific ways and means of contact between the indigenous peoples and the Spaniards.

In these territories, frontier forts and adjacent Jesuit and Franciscan missions allowed the development of a broad range of economic relationships and martial cooperation. Chieftains of groups near the establishments were named officials of the crown, received their staff of office as governors and cooperated with the Spaniards against the northern Mapuche. In turn they were protected from the incursions and mischief of the rebels. Referred to as "Indian Friends," they formed troops commanded by captains. Another institution created later and which survived the colonial period was that of the "Commissars of Nations," plenipotentiaries and

interpreters who acted as virtual ambassadors and emissaries to the indigenous groups. Their presence was instrumental to the conduct of periodic parleys ("juntas") which celebrated accords or resolutions which were seldom kept.

One of the Spanish contributions having the greatest impact on the Mapuche way of life and on the continuance of the Arauco War was the horse. Obtained at first, with great difficulty from the Spaniards, and later in great numbers through trade with ethnic groups across the Andes, the horse was rapidly incorporated into the indigenous way of life. It became the Mapuche's primary military asset in times of war and gave them unprecedented mobility.

Warfare became the Mapuche's way of life. Through warfare the males obtained prestige, wealth and women. Outstanding warriors due to their abilities, manner of living and complete dedication - were the so-called "Fronterizos" south of the Bío-Bío river. The "Imperiales," on the other hand, occupying the Cautín region, were more sedentary and pacific, although they assisted the war effort by contributing soldiers and arms.

"Brave chief Catrileo and his family" (1863) (D. Honorato). Photograph courtesy of Museo Histórico Nacional.

Chief Lloncón (XIX century). Photograph courtesy of Museo Histórico Nacional.

Mapuche woman with ancient silver jewlery. Photograph courtesy of Museo Histórico Nacional.

Military alliances were frequent and the role played by the Pehuenche, who inhabited the Andean slopes, was extremely important. Dedicated to hunting and gathering, the Pehuenche were semi-nomadic, with only temporary settlements as befits an extremely warlike people. The Pehuenche played the preponderant role in defending the Bío-Bío frontier.

The Arauco War forced the Mapuche to organize efficiently, not only for offense, but for defense against continual attacks by the Spaniards. The election of a warrior chief (*toki*) on the basis of leadership and tactical abilities, provided the necessary martial cohesion when a significant conflict developed. The toki, bringing various groups, and at times whole regions, under his war banner, commanded blind obedience. Once the danger disappeared, however, the toki's authority ceased and peacetime institutions reassumed control. Mapuche martial enterprises, so startling to the Spaniards because of the organization involved, cannot be understood without an appreciation of the toki. Circumstantial solidarity in time of war materialized in the construction of forts by the Mapuche described by the chroniclers of the sixteenth and seventeenth centuries as accommodating hundreds of warriors and their families in times of danger.

Invariably, when a conflict ended , a parley was conducted, attended by representatives of the Spaniards and the Mapuche. Peace agreements were reached, travel and trade conditions and specific boundaries established. Celebrated with great pomp and circumstance, accompanied by festivities and the exchange of gifts, the meetings ended in the signing of documents faithfully embodying the agreements reached. It was unrealistic, however, to believe that the representatives of the indigenous peoples had coercive power over their people to impose respect for such commitments. In times of peace the chiefs (*lonko*) no longer represented their groups and had very limited influence over them, a circumstance which produced new frictions and motivated new confrontations.

Thus the bloody confrontations of the Arauco War continued for a period of almost three centuries. Efforts to subjugate the Mapuche were useless. Priests, military men and representatives of the Spanish crown sent periodic reports to the homeland attempting to justify maintenance of the Arauco army. Books were written, such as «Desengaño y Reparo de la Guerra del Reino de Chile» (Disillusion and Doubt about the War in the Kingdom of Chile) by Alonso González de Nájera,

43

«Cautiverio Feliz y Razón de las Guerras Dilatadas de Chile» (Pleasant Captivity and the Reason for the Prolonged Wars in Chile) by Pineda y Bascuñán, Ercilla's «La Araucana,» (The Araucana), Oña's «Arauco Domado» (Arauco Mastered) and many more in which attempts were made to explain the tenacious Mapuche resistance and to design strategies and tactics to overcome it. It was only toward the end of the nineteenth century that the republican government of Chile managed to completely pacify the Mapuche and extend national sovereignty to fully incorporate the rebellious territory between the Bío-Bío and Toltén rivers. The area now known as the Lake Region (south of Araucanía) underwent a different process. After

relations with the indigenous peoples in those territories and the presence of established military and missionary enclaves, a process of European occupation and colonization began, ending with the arrival of foreign immigrants in the mid-nineteenth century.

With the completion of the "conquest of Araucanía," the process of colonizing and ceding title to the indigenous lands began. Mapuche families were settled on surplus lands. The rise in population of the Mapuche in the twentieth century caused an exaggerated division of the land within each community, producing extremely small farmholdings and consequently, economic and social problems.

Mapuche girl. (XIX century).
Museo Chileno de Arte Precolombino.

FAMILY AND SOCIAL ORGANIZATION

"Kupël'wegne mai, Pagni-em"
Pipatueneu Amoiantü-em.
¿Chumgnechi kai petuaiyu yu pëñeñ-em
mai?
Kullkulltullegne mai, Marilúan-em
Petuam yu pëñeñ:
wentru gnei, piam,
Demo gnei, piam
Ngayu pëñeñ-em;
wentru gnei, domo gnei
nga yu pëñeñ.

Mapuche family. Museo Chileno de Arte Precolombino.

"Make a cradle, Pangui,"
Amoiante came to tell me.
How can we have more children?
What's our baby going to live on?
Fix a horn to blow, Maril'uan.
So we can have children.
It's a boy, they say.
It's a girl, they say.
The one we're going to have;
It's a boy; it's a girl
The one we're going to have.

(IN PADRE FÉLIX DE AUGUSTA, 1934)

Mapuche family.
Engraving by Gay (1854).

When a visitor approaches a *ruka* (Mapuche dwelling), barking dogs announce his arrival. Curious children come out to investigate the presence of the stranger and run to carry the news to their mother. The visitor is invited in, offered a drink and a place by the constantly burning fire. In summer, a place is set at a table in the shade of an apple tree, where he may savor the fresh and biting taste of apple cider.

Those unacquainted with Mapuche customs are astonished by the order and cleanliness which rules the household, the manners and obedience of the small children and the easy, smooth manner in which family life takes place.

The woman is in constant motion, caring for her children, preparing food, engaged in other domestic tasks. She must care for her garden and several kinds of small animals (i.e., rabbits, chicken, geese). In quiet moments, she uses a distaff to spin wool from sheep shearings or to weave the yarn into colorful ponchos, blankets, sashes and other textiles. Ceramics and basket-weaving are also feminine responsibilities, accomplished inside the house during the winter and outside in warmer months. In all these tasks the mistress of the household is assisted by her youngest children as well as her unmarried daughters, who receive a valuable education in preparation for the time when they marry, leave their home and begin a new family in their husband's *ruka*.

The head of the household is the man. His day-to-day work is outside the house, related to farming and caring for his cattle and horses. The Mapuche men also excel in woodcarving and in producing leather crafts.

In summer, family life takes place in the open air. The small ones play near the *ruka*. The adolescents take care of the animals. The father and mother work at their day-to-day tasks. In the winter, while the rain falls incessantly on the straw roof, the family gathers around the fire and, ignoring the smoke that fills the ruka and blackens its walls, carry out, in the intimacy of the home, a cultural process of fundamental importance: while the women work unceasingly at domestic tasks, the older members of the family entertain themselves with long conversations and discourses about their oral history, their ancestors and the deeds attributed to them. Thus the children, who silently and attentively observe this scene on a daily basis, absorb their cultural heritage. These moments provide instruction for the small ones in Mapuche standards of etiquette, morality and manners.

For a Mapuche family, sons repesent continuance. They marry and establish homesteads on their father's lands; they assist their parents as long as they live, and then inherit the land. Daughters, on the other hand, live with their parents only until they marry. They then leave their parents' home

Woman by her outdoor fireplace (M. Thomas).

Mapuche woman grinding corn (M. Thomas).

*Mapuche woman next to her fireplace in her **ruka** (M. Thomas).*

and establish residence in the home of their husband. Their children belong to their husband's lineage and lose all claim to maternal land.

Kinship ties are in accordance with the male lineage. Thus, a young man calls the children of his father's brother "brothers" or "sisters" and marriage to such a "sister" is forbidden as incestuous. Marriage between crossed cousins (daughter of the brother with the son of the sister), however, is a tie to be sought and, in earlier times, an obligatory alliance.

As the unmarried members of a residential group are linked among themselves by paternal lineage, young men must seek mates outside the community. This type of marriage is called exogamic.

Once the intended spouse has been located, and the courting, which consists of periodic visits by the boy to the girl's settlement - particularly during social or ritual occasions - has taken place, the boy's father, having been impressed with his son's desires, and approving his choice, will send a *werken* (messenger) to the girl's home to negotiate a commitment. The terms settled, the bridegroom's family and friends visit the bride's home on a pre-established date, bringing money, animals, adornments and silverware. If the owners of the home are satisfied with the amount and quality of the gifts, the couple contract matrimony in a solemn ceremony which evolves into a party. The father of the bride showers her with gifts, which may include his best horse. After a few days, the new couple will receive a visit from the parents of the bride, who bring bread and flour. After some time, a new house is constructed for the couple, close by the home of the bridegroom's father.

A friendly talk (M. Thomas).

50

Mapuche women (XIX century). Photograph courtesy of Museo Histórico Nacional.

*Mapuche woman carrying her child in a **cupulhue**, or cradle (M. Thomas).*

Mapuche woman (M. Thomas).

In the old form of marriage by abduction, which is no longer practiced, the bridegroom, his parents and friends would steal the selected woman from the home of her parents and, after the marriage was consummated, make sacramental offerings to her parents. At times the abduction was simulated, but it was often carried out without the consent of the bride's parents and brothers, and even without the bride's consent, which sometimes sparked a true battle.

Polygamy, the marriage of one man with various women, was common among earlier Mapuche families. Even today there is talk of ancestors with many wives who are considered a symbol of power and wealth. Usually a man would marry the sisters of his first wife, which allowed for greater understanding among them. Rigorous rules of etiquette and organization impeded the frictions which could arise in polygamous marriages. Each woman was assigned a specified part of the house and had her own fireplace where she cooked for herself and her progeny. She had a separate garden and raised her own animals. The first wife had the greatest status and the others had to obey her orders. Often it was the first wife who would ask the husband to bring home a younger woman because she felt too old and tired and needed assistance in running the household. Economic pressure on modern Mapuche and the influence of Western customs, particularly Christianity, caused polygamy to die out.

A grouping of various families connected by paternal lineage form a community which generally inhabits a commonly-owned territory. Spatially, however, Mapuche settlements do not form village clusters, as they are more or less disperse. Each family lives in its own ruka surrounded by its own corrals, gardens and lands that it utilizes. It appears that this manner of land use pre-dates the Spanish conquest, as it was described by the first conquistadors as characteristic of the region.

Family relationships, spatial proximity and ties of cooperation and loyalty keep the families who form a local group united. Religious beliefs also are of vital importance to the relationship of the members of each community. Ancestors and founders of paternal lineages are elevated to divinities and rendered religious homage that is shared closely by all the families of a clan.

The exchange of women, necessitated by the exogenous matrimonial system, is one of the most powerful vehicles linking the various Mapuche clans and an element of basic importance for understanding Mapuche society. Such economic activities as agricultural works and the construction of houses, as well as the organization of inter-clan competitions and sporting events including chueca or *palin* (an indigenous game similar to field hockey), are based upon maternal lineage relationships. Vitally important, too, at this level of social and cultural integration of Mapuche society, is the role played by religious institutions, standards and values, in maintaining social cohesion.

*Amphora or **messen** (XIX century) Museo Chileno de Arte Precolombino (n°1458) (F. Maldonado).*

POLITICAL
ORGANIZATION

Chewül lonko meu
futa trapial reké
petu niekai newen
Tañi ange lif ngei
Ka ngenopayungei
Tañi ñapaz lonko
Kurüngei
femngekei ñi ad
futa küme che
Anai, papai, papai.

*Chiefs with their symbols in an **awun** ceremony (M̱. Thomas).*

His head,
arrogant like the lion's
still has strength.
His face is clean and
beardless, his hair is soft
and black.
Such is the contenance of a
great chief,
oh mother, my mother!.

(IN P.F. DE AUGUSTA, 1934)

Stone flute (X-XV century)
Museo Chileno de Arte
Precolombino (n°216)
(F. Maldonado).

The Mapuche conceive of family organization as patriarchal - the patriarch, of course, being the man, the head of the family. His opinions and decisions are accepted without discussion. He represents the interests of the family in the clan.

In pre-Hispanic eras, the basic authority within the extended family or clan which made up a local grouping was held by the *lonko* (head), the most prestigious male. The *lonko* was also usually the *ülmen* (richest man). The authority and ascendence of the *lonko* over other members of the group was based on his riches, good judgment and eloquence.

Other than the economic advantages of being the *ülmen* - reflected in a larger *ruka* and a greater number of wives - the chief's life was very similar to that of the other members of the family. His prudence as *lonko* in relating to subordinates was

fundamental. Any decision affecting the community was subject to acceptance by the other heads of households. Autocratic attitudes were not accepted. In the planting and harvesting of his fields, the lonko was assisted by the entire group, an occasion called *lof kudau*, when he lavished his people with entertainment, reaffirming his prestige within the group and redistributing his riches.

Social cohesion, then, was not merely dependent upon the chief but, principally, upon the close family ties which united the clan and to the solidarity and cooperation growing out of those links. The pattern of dispersed population, the great mobility of the groups and the possibility that they might disagree with the chief's authority, form another group and move away, combined to weaken subordination to the *lonko*.

Manta of a Mapuche chief, Museo Chileno de Arte Precolombino, (loan from Isabel Baixas).

*Chief making an offering on **ngillatun** altar (M. Thomas).*

The Spanish conquest introduced modifications in the Mapuche social organization. The conquistadors, to strengthen the empire they were establishing, imposed greater social stratification on conquered territories. The Spanish crown even named chiefs governors and administrators, giving them scepters as symbols of authority in the name of the King. That situation also applied to some regions south of the Toltén river, where the Spaniards established military and missionary enclaves.

The impact of war on Araucanía obliged the indigenous inhabitants of the land to establish a stronger, more cohesive social system to wage war: the toki (war chief), an institution which lasted no longer than the duration of the conflict for which the *toki* was elected.
The system of reservation settlements imposed by the Chilean State after "pacifying" the indigenous territories produced a greater dependence on the chief, who was given the authority to divide the land among the members of his community. The traditional social system, however, did not change greatly. Decisions which affect the interests of the community are still taken in consultation with all of the more prestigious members of the group.

This reservation system has made each community into a unit and established different pressure groups in each, making unity among Mapuche, as well as the development of their territories, more difficult.

Recent policies of dividing common territories among the families of each reservation will contribute to a greater social and political disintegration of Mapuche society. Today, the Chilean authorities are studying a new law aimed at protecting Mapuche traditions within the framework of a modern national economy.

Mapuche man.
Photograph courtesy
Museo Histórico Nacional.

THE ECONOMY
AND THE ARTS

Deume yu niewel koni yu trur kudawn
Inche keramapukefun kill ketran
tëkukefun,
welu pichike mëten
Fei ruka meu mëlekequi, fill
deumaniekefui
feichi iaquel ka feichi duwen kai

Mapuche family in summertime. Photograph courtesy of Museo Histórico Na[...]

"After we were married we both worked.
I plowed and sowed a little bit of everything.
She stayed at home, made all kinds of food,
and also devoted time to spinning and weaving."

(IN W. DE MOESBACH, 1930)

Pifillkas, *or vertical whistles.*
Museo Chileno de Arte
Precolombino (n°1353,1359)
(F. Maldonado).

In pre-Hispanic times, the Mapuche subsisted by hunting, fishing and collecting shellfish, as well as by gathering a rich variety of plant items. Most likely the man, in the company of his male relatives, hunted guanacos, small deer and other animals. The women, accompanied by their children, went to the woods in search of wild fruit such as *maqui, boldo*, "murta," strawberries and *cóguil*, from which they prepared fresh and fermented beverages, and wild herbs, including *yuyos*, thistles, *nalcas* and different ferns, to make soups seasoned with red peppers and grease. In the foothills of the Andes, the main economic activity, after hunting, was the collection of pine nuts, the principal source of food for the indigenous peoples of that region.

The *lafkenche* ("inhabitant of the coast") turned to the sea at low tide to gather sea urchins, mussels, razor clams and crabs. The women collected *collof* (a brown alga) and its roots (known as *huilte*), *luche* (sea lettuce) and *lúa*. Fishing was a community effort practiced by dragging large nets woven of vegetable fibre. Individual fishermen used harpoons and tridents made of *coligüe* (an indigenous cane).

The *weke* (llama or **Lama glama**), later called *chiliweke* to distinguish it from European sheep, was domesticated by the Mapuche, although in reduced numbers, as compared with the herds of the Central Andes. The possession of *wekes* was a symbol of wealth and aristocracy among the Mapuche, and their wool, the only fiber available for making textiles, much appreciated. There is no indication that *wekes* were used by indigenous Mapuche for transportation.

The cultivation of land was limited to the maintenance of small family gardens with beans, lima beans, *dawe* (a cereal), pumpkins, peppers and potatoes. Small fields were laboriously cleared in the forests to cultivate *wa* (corn).

Shucking corn (M. Thomas).

The subsistence nature of these tasks caused Mapuche groups to move from place to place in search of better lands with more plentiful food resources.

This mobility favored interaction between the groups inhabiting the different ecological niches. Those occupying the plains (*lelfunche*) traveled to the coast to exchange their grains for marine products. Salt and *pewen* nuts gathered by the Pehuenche in the foothills of the cordillera were highly valued commodities in the valley.
By the process of conquest and colonization, Europeans introduced exotic vegetable and animal species which adapted to the new world and were readily adopted by the indigenous peoples. Outstanding among them were wheat and barley as cultivated crops and sheep, horses and cattle as domestic animals. Apple trees adapted so well to the climate of Araucanía that in a few years they formed veritable forests. Called *manshana* by the indigenous peoples, the apple took its place as a staple gathered in the forest.

Gathering pine nuts in an araucaria forest (M. Thomas).

While the aboriginal population of the pacified regions, in an accelerated process of "mestizaje" (racial and cultural mixing), adopted a new mode of life dictated by the demands of agriculture, the non-pacified natives of the southern regions retained their traditional mobility, accelerated now by the Araucanian War and the introduction of the horse. The development of agricultural activities was limited to the adoption of new species. On the other hand, herding activities, as befitted their nomadic life style, increased with the introduction of goats, sheep, horses and cattle. During the colonial period, horses and cattle crossed the Andes with the Pehuenche and became an important trade item with Spanish merchants who went into Araucanía looking for cattle to sell in the markets of cities such as Chillán and Los Angeles.

After the "pacification" of Araucanía, with the indigenous peoples restricted to the reservations granted them by the Chilean State, a closer, more permanent tie was created between the Mapuche and the land. The gathering of forest products was gradually replaced by agricultural activities.

Herds penned until daybreak (N. Piwonka).

Ruka (B. Borowicz).

Only since the early part of this century did the Mapuche have what could be properly called an agricultural economy. Although limited by their economic condition, they have absorbed the techniques of cultivation, crop rotation, and managing draft animals used by their peasant counterparts. Fertilizers and farm machinery are accessible only to a very limited number of communities. Sowing and harvesting techniques are not always appropriate for soil conservation and increased production.

A large part of the land ceded to Mapuche communities is hilly and should be terraced or contour plowed before planting. The ideal use for this land would be to cultivate forestry resources. Mapuche, however, who must work this land intensively for subsistence, are unaware of these techniques and have accidentally caused accelerated erosion, which has progressed to a disastrous state in the case of lands belonging to coastal communities.

The tradition of *lof kudau* (group labor) persists for certain agricultural tasks such as sowing and harvesting on the lands of some prominent personage of the community, who convokes his relatives and friends to work his lands during times of special needs, and rewards them with festivities.

Chañuntuku (textile saddle). This article represents the synthesis of equestrian and textile art - both fundamental aspects of Mapuche life. Museo Chileno de Arte Precolombino (F. Maldonado).

Woman weaving on a vertical loom, or witral (N. Piwonka).

Earlier, during the harvesting of wheat, the major Mapuche crop during the post-Hispanic period, threshing was accomplished by staging a large dance during which couples danced on the wheat stalks to the sounds of *kultrun* (drums) and *pifillka* (whistles). Even today harvest time is cause for celebration and an increase in the visits among relatives as well as an improvement in the quality of foods and the consumption of great quantities of meat.

Other tasks employing *lof kudau* or *mingaco* (communal labor) are those that benefit the entire community, such as the cleaning of canals, construction and repair of roads and bridges and the preparation of the fields, a ritual celebrated with fertility rites.

Less frequent is the *rukan* or house raising, an occasion for long, colorful "fiestas."

The *ruka* of earlier times appears to have been of enormous dimensions, covering 120 to 240 square meters (1300 to 2600 square feet), sheltering an

Makuñ,or warp-tie dyed manta. Museo Chileno de Arte Precolombino (n°1720) (F. Maldonado).

extended family group which included a large number of relatives, and was constructed by all the residents of a community. Once the ground was prepared, the post holes were dug and the shape of the *ruka* outlined. The neighbors then cut beech beams, pulled up saplings and straw and wove them together with vines to raise the walls which were then covered with rattan wickerwork. Thick vegetation covering the walls and roof provided first class insulation against inclement weather. This type of construction, cool in summer and easy to heat in winter, is still preferred in some localities.

Entering the *ruka*, one distinguishes various sections. Inside, opposite the entrance, is a storage area for pitchers of *chicha* (fermented fruit juice) and *mudai* (corn liquor), sacks of grain and trunks with clothes and utensils. In the central area is the open fireplace, with beds to each side and strings of pepper and corn hanging from the rafters. The entrance is generally oriented toward the east and it is there that the woman installs her *witral* (loom) for weaving during the winter. Vent holes-*ullon-ruka* - at

each end of the roof allow the smoke from the fire to escape.

The *ruka* is the setting for most of the Mapuche woman's daily activities. This is where she makes her household pottery - pots, cups and dishes - grinding up clay and mixing it with *uku* to give it consistency, dampening and kneading the resultant mixture to produce a long modeling strip, coiling the strip over a base to fashion the desired piece, and finally, burnishing and firing the article to achieve the final product.

In her spare time, she spins yarn from sheep's wool. With her spindle and distaff, she produces yarns of various thicknesses, depending on the cloth to be manufactured. In the dyeing process, she uses *relvun* to obtain different shades of red, *maqui* or mud for blacks, and *collof* alga or *radal* for browns, in addition to store-bought, artificial dyes. To weave blankets, mantas, mats and rugs, she employs a vertical loom, carefully distributing the complicated designs and symbols handed down from generation to generation. Finer weaves, including textured

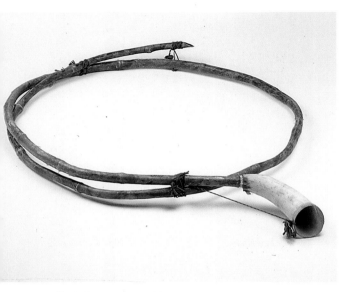

Trutruka, or trumpet, Museo
Chileno de Arte Precolombino
(nº1664) (F. Maldonado).

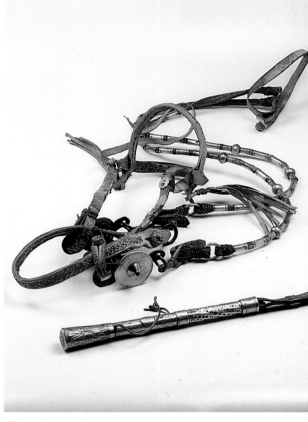

Silver adorned riding gear.
Private collection (F. Maldonado).

cloths and men's and women's sashes, are woven on a horizontal loom, set on the ground, similar to the kind used in the Central Andes.

Masculine activities, on the other hand, are generally outside the *ruka*. The man works with wood, utilizing the adze, making tiles, various kinds of instruments and all types of artifacts for domestic use, such as benches, plates and receptacles.

Mapuche statuary is principally of wood and includes the *rewe*, ceremonial stairs used by the shamans, the anthropomorphic *ngillatúe* which represent deities and preside over fertility rites, and *mamulche*, funeral statues which may represent the deceased. Musical instruments fashioned from horns and wood are the *pifillka* (whistle), *kultrun* (drum) and *trutruka* (trumpet). There are very few metalworkers, but those who work in silver merit special mention for their ability and creativity in the fabrication of women's jewelry, including rings, bracelets, headbands, combs, chest pieces and brooches, as well as saddle decorations and riding gear, the main pride of a chieftain or powerful man in Araucanía.

These handicrafts have suffered a decline with the access of the Mapuche to urban markets, such as in the modern city of Temuco, which provide easy to obtain substitutes. Thus, such products as the mans' *chamal* and *chiripa*, and the woman's *kepan* (distinctive Mapuche clothing which consisted of handloomed cloth) were rapidly replaced by the products of urban industry. The urge to imitate has not only influenced Mapuche dress but resulted in the adoption of new utensils for domestic use as well, causing the disappearance of traditional artifacts. Mapuche textile arts, however, persist, as handwoven mantas, blankets, *lama* (fringed cloths) and small mats offer quality which has not been matched by industrial production. Due to economic strife, many Mapuche families have had to the sell off their traditional silver jewelry - highly sought - after by collectors.

Ispuela, *or silver spur,*
Museo Chileno de Arte
Precolombino (nº1331).

Tralal-tralal, *or ornamental*
silver brooch, Museo Chileno de
Arte Precolombino (nº1236).

Sequil, *or ornamental silver*
breastplate, Museo Chileno de
Arte Precolombino (nº1200).

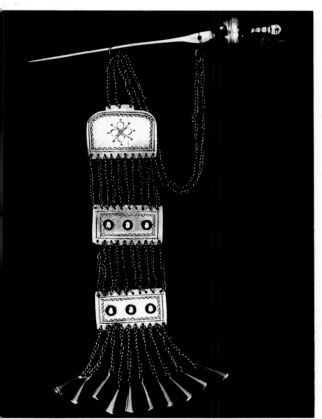

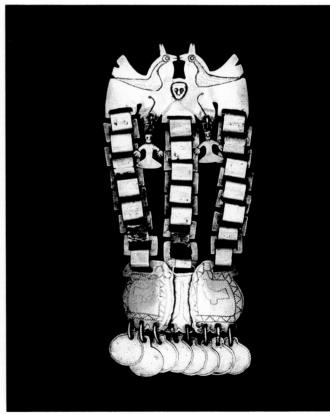

GOOD AND EVIL

Piku mapu pi am,
Tuullei na wekufu
Pa pülli na rupai
Raniñ wenu rupai.

Cementery (XIX-XX century). Photograph courtesy of Museo Histórico Nacional.

From the North, they say,
Came the demon.
Under the ground he passed,
Through the air he passed.

(IN PADRE FÉLIX DE AUGUSTA, 1934)

Gualuchos or metal anthropomorfic figures, Museo Chileno de Arte Precolombino, loan from Benjamín Lira (F. Maldonado).

To explain itself and its world, formulate judgments and order its values, Mapuche culture carries a rich load of beliefs, as well as a variety of rites which allow man to put himself in contact with the forces of nature and the supernatural. The *machi* (shaman), who contacts and mediates between these two worlds, plays a basic role in this cosmological system.

The celestial region (*Wenu mapu*) holds a plenitude of gods who occupy distinct positions in a well-established hierarchy. At the apex of the pantheon is a personage now designated with the name of *Ngenemapun* ("owner of the land") or *Ngenechen* ("master of men"). This king of gods possesses two pairs of opposing attributes: masculine-feminine sex and youth-old age, which give rise to his four personalities: The Old Man, The Old Woman, The Youth and The Girl. This supreme being led the Mapuche to the place they now inhabit and eternally oversees their well-being. He lives in an indeterminate place in the upper regions of the sky.

Some celestial bodies, such as the moon (*Killén*), the morning star (*Wuñelf*) and the stars (*Wanglén*) are deified as well and bring their influence to bear directly on the *machi* (shaman), whose gifts of foresight and magic depend on these astral beings. Ceremonial prayers solicit the intercession of fallen heroes who have reached mythic heights. Thus, they invoke the spirits of past warriors, chieftains and revered *machis*. Ancestors and the founders of lineages have also come to occupy a place in *Wenu mapu*, the celestial world, and are expected to continue to oversee the safety and prosperity of

Ritual prayer field or cancha, (B. Borowicz).

*Ngillatun ceremony in the **inapire mapu.***

their descendents, just as they did in life. These spirits often present the same pair of opposing aspects as described for the supreme being, so that, in prayer, it is customary to invoke The Old *Machi* Man, The Old *Machi* Woman, The Young *Machi* Male and The Young *Machi* Female. The same is done with the other mythic beings, as well as with the ancestors.

The spirits of glorified ancestors are personified in the *Pillan*, who lives behind the mountains, in the East, or *puel mapu*. Invocation of the *Pillan*, the supernatural being closest to man, constitutes the first rung on the ascent toward the sacred world.

Natural forces, intimately linked to beliefs, have given mythic connotation to the land's various parts. Two points of the compass are related to Good: the South, the keeper of good winds which bring fair weather, good fortune and abundance; and the East, abode of the *Pillan*, the place most charged with religious significance. That is why the *ruka* usually faces East. The *ngillatue* (anthropomorphic figures), which preside over

ngillatun (prayer ceremonies), are also oriented toward the eastern mountains; their line of sight must remain unobstructed during the entire ceremony . *The machi* installs her *rewe* (ladder to heaven) in such a manner that, while looking at the statues, she directs her prayers to the East.

The colors of the sky - blue and white - are charged with positive values and are related to sacred objects. *Machi* banners or flags only feature these colors. Sacred statues are decorated with two parallel lines, blue and white, painted below the eyes and across the nose. Participants in the *ngillatun* dance paint their faces in the same manner. At such times it is considered good taste to dress in clothing which has the same colors.

The *folie*, or cinnamon tree, is worshipped as the embodiment of divine attributes and messenger of peace. The *maqui* (a shrub with sweet, edible berries), the laurel and the apple tree also assume these characteristics, and their use is frequent in the decoration of religious places and objects, in *machi* rites and prayers.

Ngillatun *ritual dancers. Photograph courtesy of Museo Histórico Nacional.*

Kollon, *or ritual mask, Museo Chileno de Arte Precolombino, (nº1829) (F. Maldonado).*

Stone pipes (X-XVIII century), Museo Chileno de Arte Precolombino (nº1344, 1602) (F. Maldonado).

With the influence of Christianity, much of the diversity and dualistic nature of Mapuche deities has been lost, causing the religious system to become more monotheistic. At the present time, the supreme being is referred to as *Chau Dios* (a combination of Mapuche and Spanish meaning "God the Father"), creator or master of man and the earth. The customary paired oppositions of attributes are still found, however, in the songs and prayers of the *machi*, ritual elements which as a result of being handed down from generation to generation, remain largely unchanged in structure as well as content.

These same outside influences have produced confusion among the Mapuche themselves with respect to the *Pillan*, which some conceive of as a deity and others as a demon. The *Pillan* was presumably characterized as a demon by the missionaries because of his abode in a region of volcanoes and his attributes of governing and being represented by eruptions, lightning, thunder and other catastrophic elements.

The world of evil, of occult and demonic forces, is found below the earth (*Nag mapu*), a region inhabited by monstrous beings and animals which feed upon human flesh or blood. The color associated with *Nag mapu* is black, and the forces which predominate are disgrace, sickness, death, bad luck and misery.

The geographic location associated with *Nag mapu* is the North, the source of the evil wind which ruins harvests. The West, where the sun hides and the souls of the dead abide, is also viewed with fear and distrust.

This world of evil is populated by a series of mythical anthropological and zoomorphic beings (*wekufu*) who visit the world of the Mapuche to sow misfortune, calamity and death. *Witranalwe*, represented as a tall, skeletal man presaging misfortune, gallops through fields by night dressed in a long, black manta, attacking men. Anyone who associates with *Witranalwe* becomes rich with ease, but is condemned to stay with him forever. *Witranalwe* is greatly feared and often seen in the darkness of the fields.

The restless spirit of a dead girl, if awakened by a witch, may rise from her grave and become the witch's ally and accomplice. This *Anchimallen* may be recognized by its incandescent eyes, which glow like coals.

The Ñakiñ (infant), a ghost which attracts travelers into a swamp with his cry, and the *Chon-chon* (a winged witch's head) are other figures in this group of human-faced monsters.

Mythological animals who people the world include the *Piwichen* (a feathered serpent), *Ngurru* vilu (a serpent-tailed fox), *Wallipeñ* (a deformed sheep) and others, all of which suck the blood or breath from human beings, causing them to die by consumption. The *Cherrufe* is a type of meteorite which crosses the heavens announcing impending catastrophes.

There are persons linked to the subterranean world of evil: *kalku* (witches) who have the power to invoke the assistance of the *wekufu* in their nefarious undertakings. In general they are female and live far from their clans, in the midst of woods, preferably in caves (*renu*). Mapuche show great fear and loathing for *kalku* but, on occasion, secretly consort with them to solicit their cooperation.

These black magic professionals inherit their art from their ancestors or acquire it through long periods of apprenticeship. Old women, widowed or unmarried, who live apart and behave strangely are considered *kalku* by their neighbors. It is believed that they meet secretly to celebrate strange and macabre rites in certain deep, dark *renu*.

For the Mapuche, death and sickness do not have natural causes. They are the result of the action of evil forces acting upon a person. Normally, a *wekufu* or *kalku* is blamed for provoking such evil forces. Should it be a *wekufu*, the *machi* will exorcise the demon from the victim's body. If a *kalku*, the evil witch must be discovered and accused. In ancient times a person accused of witchcraft was condemned to die on the grounds that she constituted a danger to the survival of the community. Today such persons are shunned and must migrate to new groups or live in isolation.

When a *kalku* dies, her soul does not rest peacefully in the mountains or journey to the other side of the sea to eat black potatoes with the other dead souls.

Instead it becomes a member of a band of demons, assuming the role of one of the beings described earlier, usually the *chon-chon*, until, finally, taking root in another *kalku* which will become its successor.

Stone club head with serpent and cayman representation, Museo Chileno de Arte Precolombino (n°0215).

SHAMANISM

Re
rayenllaweñmanemen,
yenemen mawida meu.
Folle rewñmanenmen,
Yenemen mawida meu,
Triwereweñmanenmen.

Machi, or shaman, next to her **rewe**, beating a **kultrun**
and playing **kashkawilla** (M. Thomas).

I was all covered with flower medicine
When they went to look for me on the
mountain.
I was covered with the sacred branches
of the cinnamon tree,
When they went to look for me on the
mountain.
I was covered with the branches of the
laurel.

(IN PADRE FÉLIX DE AUGUSTA, 1934)

Kultrun or ceremonial drum of the **machi**, *Museo Chileno de Arte Precolombino (n°2607) (F. Maldonado).*

The *machi*, or *fileu*, is the intermediary between the Mapuche people and the *Wenu mapu* (land of the gods). Through her mediation, the divinities grant health, well-being, tranquility and abundance. The *machi* is principally charged with divine representation in the daily struggle between good and evil that takes place on the earth. Thus, she is imbued with powers to divine, to cure and to conduct rituals.

According to the early chroniclers and travelers, this profession was exercised only by men endowed with sexual ambiguity, a characteristic of the gods. At the present, due to European and Christian influences, this role is mainly played by women, without any bisexual attributes.

There are a series of signs indicating that a Mapuche has been chosen to serve as a *machi*. She has visions or premonitory dreams related to certain animals that are white in color. Later she contracts an "incurable" disease which can only be alleviated by her consecration as *a machi*. Once having decided to be *a machi*, she enters into an agreement with an experienced machi for training as a student apprentice. She then constructs her *ruka* and lives alone, initiating herself into the secrets of medicinal plants and the science of the complicated rituals and ceremonies of invocation, closely supervised by her teacher. After some years of apprenticeship, she prepares for the great day of her initiation, celebrated with the solemn ceremony of *machiluwun* attended by all the well-known *machis* of the area, who will help her at this time.

The *machi* -to-be would have already carved her ceremonial *rewe* stair, symbol of her status and ability to communicate with the *Wenu mapu*. She would also have prepared a *kultrun*, the ceremonial drum to whose sound she will sing and dance the rest of her life invoking the gods and ancestors to assist her people.

Upper part of a **rewe**
or ceremonial ladder
(B. Borowicz).

Offerings on a **rewe** *(B. Borowicz).*

Machiluwun, *or **machi** ritual iniciation. Photograph courtesy of Museo Histórico Nacional.*

With the *rewe* planted in the earth to the East of her house, over ancient silver coins, all the *machis* in attendance sing to the *Wuñelfe* (morning star) invoking the *Pillan* of the East, the Old *Machis* and Warriors, the Old King, the Old Queen, the Young Warrior, the Young Maiden, the ancient and powerful Chiefs and, above all, the Moon and the Stars, to assist the new *machi*.

The *rewe* is decorated with branches of sacred kinds of trees. To each side are fixed the flags that the new *machi* has chosen as her standards, with astral symbols and representations of moons and stars in white and blue (the colors of the heavens). The attendants also prepare the body of the initiate in a complicated rite designed to make her immune to the forces of evil.

The *machiluwun* ceremony culminates with the dance and song of the initiate, who ascends for the first time the sacred steps of the *rewe*, to the sound of the *kultrun*, which she beats with her right hand, covered with bells. The climax arrives when the *machi* falls into a trance, moves with agitated convulsions which her assistants attempt to restrain, and begins to transmit the messages of the gods, which are then repeated by the *machidungun* (interpreter).

Utilizing this power of communication with the celestial beings, the new *machi* will exorcise the evil spirits which cause injuries and administer medicines in the *machitun*. During the *ngillatun*, when asking the deities for the fertility of the fields, increases in the number of animals and the well-being of the community, the *machi* will lift her eyes to the East and, to the beat of the *kultrun*, sing:

We pray for rain to produce the harvests, to multiply our animals.
Great Man with the Golden Head, and you, Great Woman, say: "Let it rain!"
We pray to the two Great, Old Persons...

Machi *and assistants playing musical instruments (M. Thomas).*

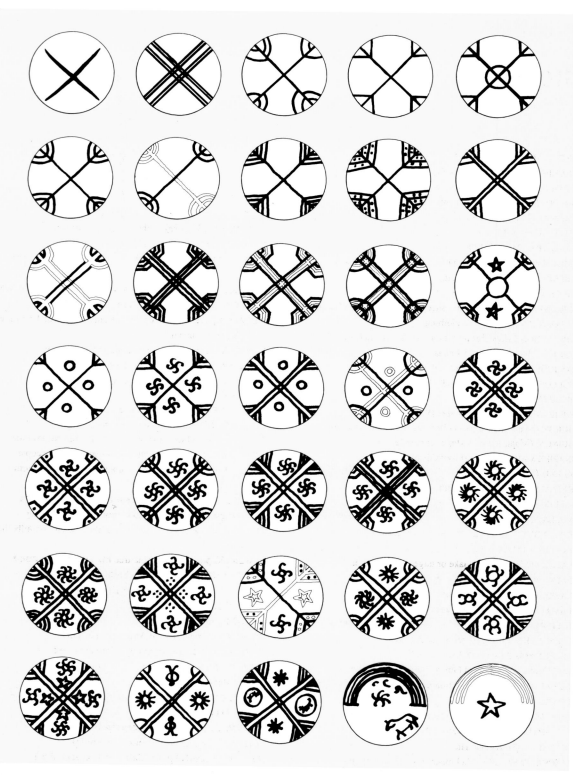

*Different drumhead designs of the **kultrun**.*
Drawing by José Pérez de Arce, Museo Chileno de Arte Precolombino.

GLOSSARY OF INDIGENOUS TERMS

ANCHI (*Mapuche*) shine

ANCHIMALLEN (*Mapuche*) mythology - girl with shining eyes

AUKA (*Quechua*) cruel enemy, evil

BOLDO (*Mapuche*) a tree (**Peumus boldus**)

CHAMAL (*Mapuche*) breechcloth

CHAU (*Mapuche*) father

CHAU DIOs (*Mapuche*) Father God

CHE (*Mapuche*) person, people

CHERRUFE (*Mapuche*) mythology -aerolite

CHICHA (*Quechua*) fermented beverage

CHILIWEKE (*Mapuche*) "earth sheep" - llama (**Lama glama**)

CHIRIPA (*Mapuche*) men's clothing

CHON-CHON (*Mapuche*) mythology - winged witch's head

COGUIl (*Mapuche*) vines **Vitaceae**

COLIGÜE (*Mapuche*) a large bamboo (**Chusquea coleu**)

COLLOF (*Mapuche*) a sea weed (**Durvillea antarctica**)

FILEU (*Mapuche*) shaman

FOLIE (*Mapuche*) cinnamon tree (**Drymis winteri**)

HUILTE (*Mapuche*) stem of collof (**Durvillea antarctica**)

HUINCA: (*Mapuche*) non-Mapuche people

INAPIRE MAPU (*Mapuche*) foothills of the Andes

KALKU (*Mapuche*) witch

KEPAM (*Mapuche*) square cloth worn by women

KILLEN (*Mapuche*) moon

KOLLA (*Quechua*) South

KOLLA SUYU (*Quechua*) Kingdom of the South

KULTRUN (*Mapuche*) drum

LAFKEN (*Mapuche*) sea, lake or large body of water

LAFKENCHE (*Mapuche*) coast dweller

LAFKEN MAPU (*Mapuche*) coast

LAMA (*Mapuche*) small blanket

LELFUN (*Mapuche*) plain

LELFUNCHE (*Mapuche*) people of the plains

LELFUN MAPU (*Mapuche*) central valley

LOF (*Mapuche*) extended family living in one place

LOF KUDAU (*Mapuche*) community work

LONKO (*Mapuche*) chief

LUA (*Mapuche*) a sea weed (**Iridaea laminoreoides**)

LUCHE (*Mapuche*) a sea weed (**Ulva lactuca**)

MACHI (*Mapuche*) shaman

MACHILUWUN (*Mapuche*) machi initiation ceremony

MACHINDUNGUN (*Mapuche*) assistant of the machi who repeats

and interprets the machi's words

MALOCA (*Mapuche*) raid or attack on enemy settlement

MAMUL (*Mapuche*) wood, tree

MAPU (*Mapuche*) land

MAPUDUNGUN (*Mapuche*) Mapuche language

MANSHANA (*Mapuche*) apple (fr. Spanish manzana)

MAQUI (*Mapuche*) a tree (**Aristotelia maqui**)

MICHAY (*Mapuche*) a **Berberis** shrub which produces berries used for dyeing yarns

MINGACO (*Quechua*) community work rewarded with festivities

MOLUCHE (*Mapuche*) warrior (acc. Latcham)

MUDAI (*Mapuche*) fermented liquor from corn, wheat, be-rries, etc.

NAG (*Mapuche*) under

NAGEL (*Mapuche*) sundown or action of going down

NAG MAPU (*Mapuche*) beneath the earth (cf. hades)

NALCA (*Mapuche*) stems of the pangue plant (**Gunnera chilensis**)

NGILLATUE (*Mapuche*) sacred wood statue

NGILLATUN (*Mapuche*) prayer ceremony

ÑAKIŇ (*Mapuche*) mythology - infant who inhabits swamps

NGENECHEN (*Mapuche*) mythology- master of the people

NGENEMAPUN (*Mapuche*) mythology - master of the earth

NGURRU (*Mapuche*) fox

NGURRU VILU (*Mapuche*) mythology - serpent-tailed fox

PALI (*Mapuche*) game of chueca, similar to field hockey

PEHUENCHE (*Mapuche*) inhabitant of the Andean foothills (from pewen)

PEWEN (*Mapuche*) native pine tree (**Araucaria araucana**)

PIFILLKA (*Mapuche*) vertical whistle

PILLAN (*Mapuche*) mythology - spirit of the ancestors

PIKUN (*Mapuche*) North

PIRE (*Mapuche*) snow

PIRE MAPU (*Mapuche*) the Andes or snow land

PIWICHEN (*Mapuche*) mythology - serpent-tailed bird

PONTRO (*Mapuche*) blanket

PUEL (*Mapuche*) East

PUELCHE (*Mapuche*) inhabitant of the eastern slopes of the Andes

PUEL MAPU (*Mapuche*) land beyond the Andes

RADAL (*Mapuche*) plant (**Lomatia dentata**)

RELVUN (*Mapuche*) plant (**Calceolaria arachnoidea**)

RENU (*Mapuche*) witches' cave

REWE *(Mapuche)* sacred wooden ladder of the machi

RUKA *(Mapuche)* house

RUKAN *(Mapuche)* communal house construction fiesta

TOKI *(Mapuche)* warrior chief

TUPU *(Mapuche)* ornamental pin used as a brooch

TRAPELACUCHA *(Mapuche)* feminine silver pectoral

TRARIKAN *(Mapuche)* warp tie-dyeing technique

TRARILONKO *(Mapuche)* silver or textile ornament that goes around the head

TRARIWE *(Mapuche)* elaborated waist sash woven on a horizontal loom

TRUTRUKA *(Mapuche)* trumpet-like musical instrument

UKU *(Mapuche)* a special kind of stone ground to be used as clay temper

ÜLMEN *(Mapuche)* rich and powerful man (men)

ULLONRUKA *(Mapuche)* holes at both end gables of the roof to allow smoke to escape from the house

VILU *(Mapuche)* snake

WAITHIF *(Mapuche)* Argentina

WALLIPEŇ *(Mapuche)* mythology - sheep (or other quadruped) with physical deformity

WANGLEN *(Mapuche)* star

WEKE *(Mapuche)* llama **(Lama glama)**

WEKUFU *(Mapuche)* mythology - demon or evil creature

WENU *(Mapuche)* sky, up

WENU MAPU *(Mapuche)* mythology - heaven

WERKEN *(Mapuche)* emissary

WILLI *(Mapuche)* South

WITRANALWE *(Mapuche)* mythology - certain maleficent anthropomorphic spirit

WUÑELFE *(Mapuche)* morning star

YUYO *(Quechua)* a weed

REFERENCES

ALDUNATE, CARLOS
1989   "Estadio alfarero en el sur de Chile (ca. 500
         a.C. - 1800 d.C.)". *Culturas de Chile;
         Prehistoria* Hidalgo *et al.* (eds), Ed. Andrés
         Bello, pp. 329-348, Santiago.

BERDICHEWSKY, BERNARDO
1971   "Fases culturales en la prehistoria de los
         araucanos de Chile". Revista Chilena de
         Historia y Geografía Nº139, pp.105-112,
         Santiago de Chile.

COOPER, JOHN
1946   "The Araucanians". *Handbook of South
         American Indians,* vol. 2, Julian Steward (ed),
         pp. 687-760, Washington.

DE AUGUSTA, PADRE FÉLIX
1934   Lecturas Araucanas. Ed. San Francisco,
         Santiago de Chile.

DE OCAÑA, FRAY DIEGO
1969   *Un Viaje Fascinante por la América Hispana
         del Siglo XVI (1599-1605).* Julio Guerrero
         Carrasco (ed). Stadium Ediciones, Madrid.

DILLEHAY, TOM
1976   "Observaciones y Consideraciones sobre
         Prehistoria y la Temprana Epoca Histórica de la
         Región Centro-Sur de Chile". *Estudios
         Antropológicos sobre los Mapuches de Chile
         Sur-Central,* pp.1-40 Universidad Católica,
         Temuco.

ERCILLA, ALONSO DE
1888   *La Araucana.* Imprenta Cervantes, Santiago.

FARON, LOUIS
1961   *Mapuche Social Structure.* University of
         Chicago Press, Urbana.

1964   *Hawks of the Sun; Mapuche morality and its
         ritual attributes.* University of Pittsburg Press,
         Pittsburg.

1968   *The Mapuche Indians of Chile.* State University
         of New York, New York.

GAY, CLAUDIO
1854   *Atlas de la Historia Física y Política de Chile,*
         t.I. E.Thunot & Ca., Paris.

GUEVARA, TOMAS
1908   *Psicología del Pueblo Araucano.* Imprenta
         Cervantes, Santiago.

1911   *Folklore Araucano.* Imprenta Cervantes,
         Santiago.

1913   *Las Ultimas Familias y Costumbres
         Araucanas.* Imprenta Cervantes, Santiago.

1929   *Chile Prehispano,* vol.1 & 2. Establecimientos
         Gráficos Balcells & Co., Santiago.

GREBE, MARIA ESTER, *et.al.*:
1973   *Cosmovisión Mapuche.* Cuadernos de la
         Realidad Nacional Nº 14, pp.46-73, Santiago.

HILGER, INEZ
1957   *Araucanian Child Life and its Cultural
         Background.* Smithsonian Institution,
         Washington.

LATCHAM, RICARDO
1928   *La Prehistoria Chilena.* Soc. Imprenta y Lit.
         Universo, Santiago.

MENGHIN, OSVALDO
1962   "Estudios de Prehistoria Araucana". *Acta
         Prehistórica* III-IV, pp.49-120, Buenos Aires.

MOESBACH, WILHELM DE
1930   *Vida y Costumbres de los Indígenas Araucanos
         en la Segunda Mitad del Siglo XIX.* Imprenta
         Cervantes, Santiago.

METRAUX, ALFRED
1942   "Le Chamanisme Araucan". *Revista del
         Instituto de Antropología de la Universidad
         Nacional de Tucumán,* Tucumán.

MOSTNY, GRETE
1971   *Prehistoria de Chile.* Editorial Universitaria,
         Santiago.

ROBLES, EULOGIO
1942   *Costumbres y Creencias Araucanas.* Ediciones
         de la Universidad de Chile, Santiago.

ROSALES, DIEGO DE
1877   *Historia General del Reino de Chile.* Imprenta
         del Mercurio, Valparaíso.

STUCHLIK, MILAN
1974   *Rasgos de la Sociedad Mapuche
         Contemporánea.* Editorial Nueva Universidad,
         Santiago.

TITIEV, MISHA
1969   "Araucanian shamanism". *Boletín del Museo
         Nacional de Historia Natural,* vol. XXX
         pp.299-312, Santiago.

DESIGN

XIMENA SUBERCASEAUX

TRANSLATION

RICHARD C. BAKER
PETER W. KENDALL

EDITORIAL WORK

FRANCISCO MENA L.